CAN YOU CRACK IT?

The Math of Codes

Written by Bill Harrod

WORLD BOOK

www.worldbook.com

Co-published by agreement between Shi Tu Hui and World Book, Inc.

Shi Tu Hui
Room 1807, Block 1,
#3 West Dawang Road
Chaoyang District, Beijing 100025
P.R. China

World Book, Inc.
180 North LaSalle Street
Suite 900
Chicago, Illinois 60601
USA

© 2026. All rights reserved. This volume may not be reproduced in whole or in part in any form without prior written permission from the publisher.

WORLD BOOK and the GLOBE DEVICE are registered trademarks or trademarks of World Book, Inc.

Library of Congress Control Number: 2025942227

Aha! Academy: Math
ISBN: 978-0-7166-7377-4 (set, hardcover)

Can You Crack It? The Math of Codes
ISBN: 978-0-7166-7384-2 (hard cover)
ISBN: 978-0-7166-7447-4 (e-book)
ISBN: 978-0-7166-7437-5 (soft cover)

Staff

Editorial

Vice President
Tom Evans

Editorial Project Coordinator
Kaile Kilner

Senior Curriculum Designer
Caroline Davidson

Curriculum Designer
Mikayla Kightlinger

Proofreader
Nathalie Strassheim

Indexer
Nathaniel Lindstrom

Graphics and Design

Senior Visual Communications Designer
Melanie Bender

Designer
Shannon Hagman

Written by Bill Harrod

Designed by Francis Paola Lea

Acknowledgments

The publishers gratefully acknowledge the following sources for photography. All illustrations were prepared by WORLD BOOK unless otherwise noted.

Jaroslav Moravcik/Shutterstock; shisu_ka/Shutterstock; spainter_vfx/Shutterstock; VAKS-Stock Agency/Shutterstock; vectorfusionart/Shutterstock

© Photo 12/Alamy 12; © Steve Taylor ARPS/Alamy 13; © Bank of Canada 9; Luringen (licensed under CC BY-SA 3.0) 19; NARA 35; NASA 37; National Archives 10; The Penn Museum 44, 45; Public Domain 4, 11, 29; © Shutterstock 3, 4, 5, 6, 7, 8, 9, 10, 11, 12, 13, 14, 15, 16, 17, 18, 19, 20, 21, 22, 23, 24, 25, 26, 27, 28, 29, 30, 31, 32, 33, 34, 35, 36, 37, 38, 39, 40, 41, 42, 43, 44, 45, 46, 47, 48

There is a glossary of terms on page 48. Terms defined in the glossary are in type that looks like *this* on their first appearance on any spread (two facing pages).

Contents

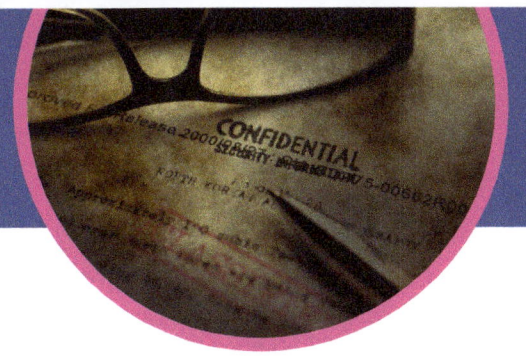

Introduction 4

① Code talking 6
  A teenager's invention 8
  Codes to the rescue! 10
  Waving flags 12

② It's a secret! 14
  Secret messages 16
  I came, I saw, I coded 18
  Swapping letters 20
  The unbreakable code (and how it was broken) . . . 22
  Pirates and buried treasure 24

③ Breaking codes 26
  Counting letters 28
  Reading Caesar's mail 30
  Read what Tut's friends wrote 32
  Codebreakers at war 34

④ Codes and computers 36
  Talking to your computer 38
  Codes at the store 40
  Are credit cards safe? 42

Write like Tut! 44
Index 46
Glossary 48

Introduction

"I use math too!"

When you hear the word "codes," what words come to mind? Spies? Secret messages? Math? You may have thought of the first two, but probably not the third.

Codes are systems of letters, numbers, or other symbols that help us *communicate* when other means of communication aren't possible or would take longer. Codes also are used to help people communicate secretly.

Math plays a vital role in making (and breaking) codes! People use math to design ways for people to communicate *efficiently*. Codebreakers use math to read enemy secrets. Codemakers use math to thwart codebreakers. Computer *programmers* use codes to tell computers what to do and to keep them safe for us to use.

1 CODE TALKING

You are probably so used to reading that you take it for granted. But what if you were blind? How would you be able to read if you couldn't see the letters and words on the page?

Codes aren't just for secret messages! They're also useful to help people *communicate* when it would otherwise be impossible for them to do so. In some cases, these codes have even saved lives!

If you want to talk with your friends, you can call them on the phone, send them a text, or email them a message. But how could you talk with people over long distances if you didn't have a phone, computer, or other electronic devices?

Let's see how math helped people design codes that allow the blind to read, made long distance communication possible, and saved people from drowning!

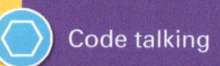

Code talking

A teenager's invention

In 1824, Louis Braille (who was only 15 years old at the time!) developed a raised dot reading system so that blind people could read by touch.

The Braille alphabet is shown below. Look at the letters a-j and k-t in the Braille alphabet. Do you notice a *pattern* (mathematicians love looking for patterns!) when you compare the letters "a" and "k," "b" and "l," etc.? You should notice that the letters k-t are the same as the letters a-j, but they have an additional dot in the lower left.

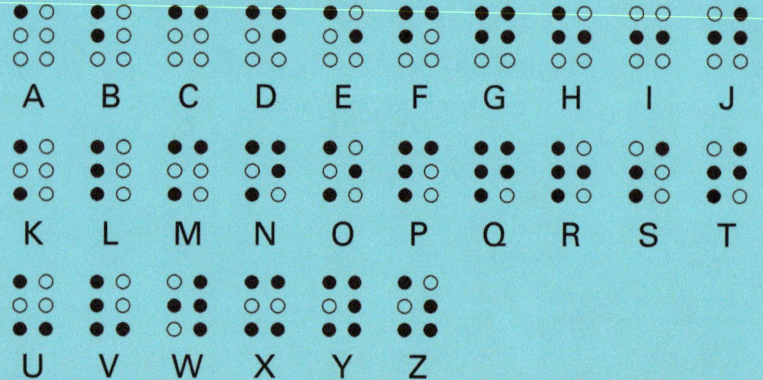

Braille Alphabet

These are the lower-case letters of the Braille alphabet. You can also indicate capital letters, numbers, and punctuation in Braille.

Close your eyes and try to read this book. Impossible, right? How can you read if you can't even see the words on the page? Imagine the difficulties blind people had .... until a teenager came up with a solution!

Using the alphabet on the other page, can you tell what this says? By the way, when no dots are raised (like here), that means that there is a space between the words.

This one says, "braille code."

Now, it is your turn. What does this one say?

This one says, "math is fun."

CURIOUS CONNECTIONS

FINANCE Some countries, including Australia, Canada, China, Egypt, India, and Russia, have currency with Braille or Braille-like markings on them to help blind and visually challenged people know how much money they have.

9

Code talking

Codes to the rescue!

Before texting, before e-mails, before the telephone, you may have used a telegraph to communicate with someone who lived far from you. A telegraph was a device that originally sent electronic signals over long wires. Later, it could send messages through radio instead of wires.

The Morse code was a system of dots (short taps) and dashes (long taps) that stood for letters of the alphabet. The International Morse Code is shown below.

In the 1840's, American inventor Samuel F. B. Morse made the first practical telegraph. Later, Morse helped develop the Morse code so that messages could be sent on the telegraph.

Imagine it's the morning of April 15, 1912, and you are on board the *Titanic*. Late the previous night, your ship hit an iceberg and is now sinking. You are in the middle of the Atlantic Ocean with no one in sight. How can you call for rescue?

If you look closely at the code, you might note that more commonly used letters (such as A, E, I, N, and T) have only 1 or 2 dots and dashes. While less commonly used letters (such as J, Q, X, and Z) have 4 dots and dashes. By giving the most common letters the fewest dots and dashes, messages can be sent more quickly because the operator is tapping out fewer dots and dashes overall.

The crew of the *Titanic* sent out one of the earliest SOS signals using Morse code (••• — — — •••) to call for help. Another ship, the *Carpathia,* heard the distress call, steamed toward the *Titanic,* and rescued hundreds of people from the frigid waters.

Use the box on the other page to determine what this says (the "/"s separate words):

— •••• •• •••/••• • —• — • —• —•—• • •• ••• •• —•
/— — — — — •—• ••• • —•—• — — — —•• •

This says, "This sentence is in Morse code."

TECH TIME

Morse Glasses help people with motion disabilities communicate. These glasses convert a person's eye blinks into dots and dashes, which are then translated into English or another language.

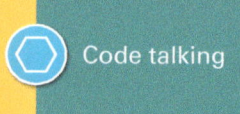 Code talking

Waving flags

In the 1790's, a French chap named Claude Chappe developed a way to quickly (for the time) relay messages. His method used towers like these with wooden "arms" that could be arranged to represent different letters, numbers, and words. French general, and later emperor, Napoleon Bonaparte used this system!

Can you think of some problems with Chappe's system? Two that come to mind are that his system could only be used in daylight and enemy units can see the towers and easily get the message.

Sometimes one idea leads to another. Let's see how coding letters using towers with long wooden beams was modified into a system of coding letters with flags.

Chappe's idea was modified into semaphore—a system of communicating with flags. Semaphore was used by navies around the world in the 1800's. While, with advances in technology, it is no longer used that much today, semaphore still can be used.

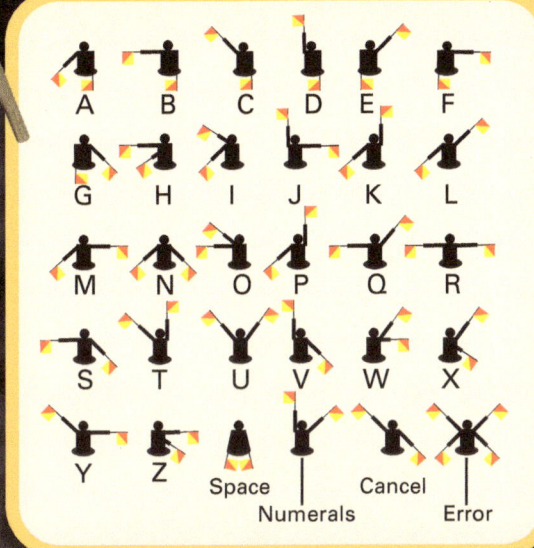

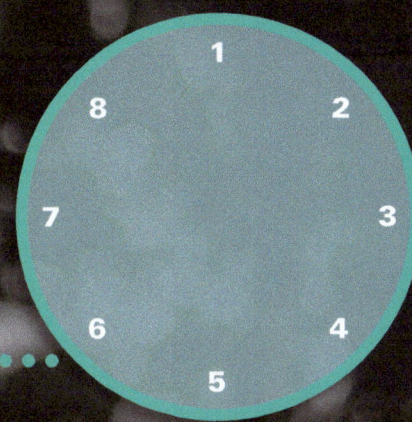

If you look at the image above, you'll notice that there are 8 different positions for each flag. Why 8? Because with 8 positions for each flag, there are 28 different ways of arranging the 2 flags (if you don't want the 2 flags in the same position)—just enough for 26-letter alphabet!

DID YOU KNOW?

The peace sign (☮) is the semaphore for the letters "n" and "d" (nuclear disarmament) placed on top of each other.

13

2
IT'S A SECRET!

Throughout history, people have used many types of secret codes to hide what their messages said. Secret codes have often been used by governments and militaries to conceal important information during critical events. And, as we will see, pirates used codes to hide buried treasure!

Imagine you are a spy! You need to send a message to your friends. But, in case the message is *intercepted,* you don't want others to know what you wrote. Maybe you could use a secret code!

Maybe you can use one of these secret codes for your own messages! Before you do, you may want to learn some of the advantages and disadvantages of these codes.

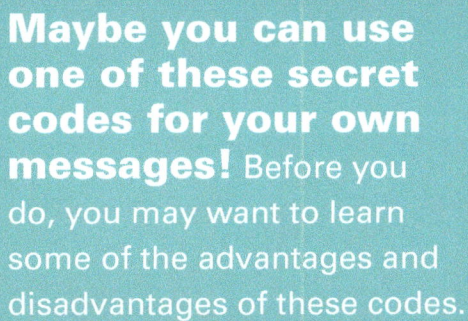

In this book, we will use the terms "plaintext" and "ciphertext." Plaintext is the original message before it is coded. Ciphertext is the message after it has been coded. Often, plaintext is written in lower case letters and ciphertext is written in capital letters. An example:

Plaintext:

> meet me at the library

Ciphertext:

> R00S R0 +S SW0 9BZL+L5

Also, while the words "code" and "cipher" have slightly different meanings, we will use the terms interchangeably in this book.

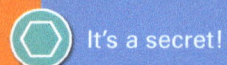
It's a secret!

Secret messages

The message says:

13 5 5 20   13 5   1 20   20 8 5   12 9 2 18 1 18 25   6 15 18   20 8 5   3 15 4 5 2 15 15 11

You open up your friend's message. What is going on here? These aren't even letters! How can you read a bunch of numbers? Maybe your friend is using the A1Z26 substitution cipher. In this cipher, "a" is replaced by "1," "b" is replaced by "2," etc. all the way to "z" being replaced by "26."

Plaintext	a	b	c	d	e	f	g	h	i	j	k	l	m	n	o	p	q	r	s	t	u	v	w	x	y	z
Ciphertext	1	2	3	4	5	6	7	8	9	10	11	12	13	14	15	16	17	18	19	20	21	22	23	24	25	26

Let's see if that helps us with her message. The 13th letter of the alphabet is "m," so that must be the first letter in her code. The other "13" in her code must also be an "m." The letter "e" is the 5th letter, so all the "5's" in her code should be replaced by "e's." If you kept replacing each number with the appropriate letter, you would get the message: **meet me at the library for the codebook**

Your friend hands you a message that she wants you to read but it is in a *secret code* in case your teacher *intercepts* it! Hopefully, she used either the A1Z26 or Atbash *cipher*. If so, we will show you how to read it!

Another type of substitution code is called the Atbash cipher. To use the Atbash cipher, you reverse the alphabet and then code a letter with its reverse. So, "a" is replaced by "Z," "b" is replaced by "Y," etc. all the way to "z" is being replaced by "A."

Plaintext	a	b	c	d	e	f	g	h	i	j	k	l	m	n	o	p	q	r	s	t	u	v	w	x	y	z
Ciphertext	Z	Y	X	W	V	U	T	S	R	Q	P	O	N	M	L	K	J	I	H	G	F	E	D	C	B	A

Our message, **"meet me at the library for the codebook"** would be coded:

NVVG NV ZG GSV ORYIZIB ULI GSV XLWVYLLP

Unfortunately, the A1Z26 and Atbash codes are easy to break and aren't actually used in real life. Also, you shouldn't pass notes in class!

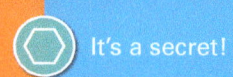
It's a secret!

I came, I saw, I coded

If you had lived in the first century B.C. and were best buds with the Roman general and politician **Julius Caesar**, he might have sent you some strange-looking messages. Caesar used a cipher (now, conveniently, called the Caesar cipher) to send important messages. If Caesar wanted to tell you "veni, vidi, vici" [Latin (Caesar's language) for "I came, I saw, I conquered"] he might have sent the message using his cipher.

Friends, scholars, codemakers, lend me your eyes! The Caesar *cipher* may be little used now, but we can still learn a lot from this historically important code

Plaintext	a	b	c	d	e	f	g	h	i	j	k	l	m	n	o	p	q	r	s	t	u	v	w	x	y	z
Ciphertext	D	E	F	G	H	I	J	K	L	M	N	O	P	Q	R	S	T	U	V	W	X	Y	Z	A	B	C

The Caesar cipher replaces each letter by another letter that is a fixed distance down (or up) the alphabet. In the example above, each letter is replaced by the letter 3 letters down the alphabet. So, the letter "a" is replaced by "D," "b" is replaced by "E," all the way through the alphabet until we get that "z" is replaced with "C."

If Caesar used this cipher, he would have replaced the "v" in "veni" with a "Y," the "e" with a "H," the "n" with a "Q," and the "i" with a "L." He would have done the same for the other 2 words. So, "veni, vidi, vici" would be coded "YHQL, YLGL, YLFL."

The main advantage to this cipher is that once you know how one letter is coded, the rest are easy to figure out. Unfortunately, that is also the code's biggest disadvantage—once someone who intercepts the message figures out one letter, they can also figure out the rest.

CURIOUS CONNECTIONS

 **HISTORY** The ancient Greeks used a scytale (a type of cylinder or stick) to send coded messages. A piece of parchment would be wrapped around the scytale, and a message written on it. When the message was unwrapped, it made no sense until the recipient wrapped it around a same-sized stick or cylinder.

19

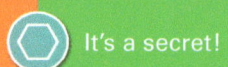

It's a secret!

Swapping letters

Substitution is a coding technique, like the Caesar cipher. The difference is that letters in the plaintext are replaced by another letter, number, or symbol that doesn't have to be a fixed number of letters down the alphabet. For example, we could use this substitution code:

Plaintext	a	b	c	d	e	f	g	h	i	j	k	l	m	n	o	p	q	r	s	t	u	v	w	x	y	z
Ciphertext	H	6	+	Q	7	D	$	L	X	R	2	A	5	T	B	Z	M	9	%	F	1	E	V	4	K	W

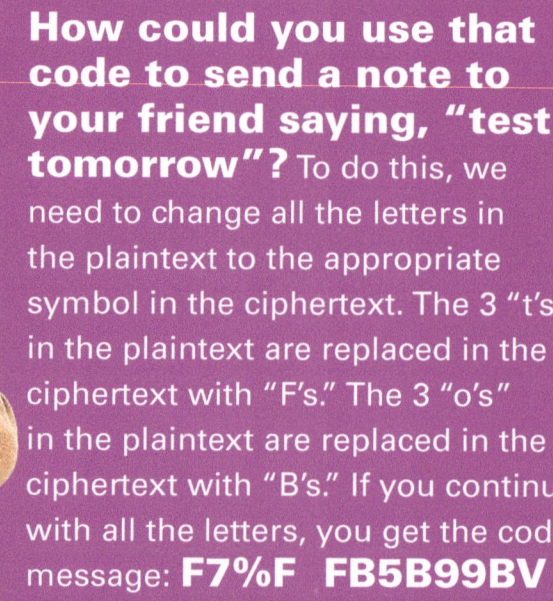

If only I learned that code, I would have known about this test!

How could you use that code to send a note to your friend saying, "test tomorrow"? To do this, we need to change all the letters in the plaintext to the appropriate symbol in the ciphertext. The 3 "t's" in the plaintext are replaced in the ciphertext with "F's." The 3 "o's" in the plaintext are replaced in the ciphertext with "B's." If you continue with all the letters, you get the coded message: **F7%F FB5B99BV**

While the A1Z26 substitution code, the Atbash cipher, and the Caesar cipher **are easy to use,** they are also easy to break. Let's try substitution—a much tougher code to break!

There is a drawback to these codes, however. Using techniques that we will learn later in the book, substitution ciphers are relatively easy to break.

Now, it is your turn. You want to send a message using the above substitution code that says, "meet me at the library." Write the message and then check it with the answer on the right.

577F 57 HF FL7 AX69H9W

CURIOUS CONNECTIONS

LITERATURE In *The Adventure of the Dancing Men*, fictional detective Sherlock Holmes **deciphered** a code where each letter was substituted with a stick figure (who sometimes held a flag) drawn in a different position.

It's a secret!

The unbreakable code (and how it was broken)

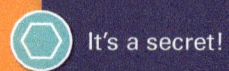

I'm not "lion" to you when I say that you picked an excellent keyword!

To use the Vigenère cipher, you must first make a table of all possible Caesar ciphers. Next, you come up with a keyword, which tells you which row to use for each letter. For example, if we choose the keyword "LION," we only use the rows with the letters, "L," "I," "O," and "N" as the first letter. Finally, we use the row with the keyword letter and the column with the plaintext letter to obtain each coded letter.

	a	b	c	d	e	f	g	h	i	j	k	l	m	n	o	p	q	r	s	t	u	v	w	x	y	z
A	A	B	C	D	E	F	G	H	I	J	K	L	M	N	O	P	Q	R	S	T	U	V	W	X	Y	Z
B	B	C	D	E	F	G	H	I	J	K	L	M	N	O	P	Q	R	S	T	U	V	W	X	Y	Z	A
C	C	D	E	F	G	H	I	J	K	L	M	N	O	P	Q	R	S	T	U	V	W	X	Y	Z	A	B
D	D	E	F	G	H	I	J	K	L	M	N	O	P	Q	R	S	T	U	V	W	X	Y	Z	A	B	C
E	E	F	G	H	I	J	K	L	M	N	O	P	Q	R	S	T	U	V	W	X	Y	Z	A	B	C	D
F	F	G	H	I	J	K	L	M	N	O	P	Q	R	S	T	U	V	W	X	Y	Z	A	B	C	D	E
G	G	H	I	J	K	L	M	N	O	P	Q	R	S	T	U	V	W	X	Y	Z	A	B	C	D	E	F
H	H	I	J	K	L	M	N	O	P	Q	R	S	T	U	V	W	X	Y	Z	A	B	C	D	E	F	G
I	I	J	K	L	M	N	O	P	Q	R	S	T	U	V	W	X	Y	Z	A	B	C	D	E	F	G	H
J	J	K	L	M	N	O	P	Q	R	S	T	U	V	W	X	Y	Z	A	B	C	D	E	F	G	H	I
K	K	L	M	N	O	P	Q	R	S	T	U	V	W	X	Y	Z	A	B	C	D	E	F	G	H	I	J
L	L	M	N	O	P	Q	R	S	T	U	V	W	X	Y	Z	A	B	C	D	E	F	G	H	I	J	K
M	M	N	O	P	Q	R	S	T	U	V	W	X	Y	Z	A	B	C	D	E	F	G	H	I	J	K	L
N	N	O	P	Q	R	S	T	U	V	W	X	Y	Z	A	B	C	D	E	F	G	H	I	J	K	L	M
O	O	P	Q	R	S	T	U	V	W	X	Y	Z	A	B	C	D	E	F	G	H	I	J	K	L	M	N
P	P	Q	R	S	T	U	V	W	X	Y	Z	A	B	C	D	E	F	G	H	I	J	K	L	M	N	O
Q	Q	R	S	T	U	V	W	X	Y	Z	A	B	C	D	E	F	G	H	I	J	K	L	M	N	O	P
R	R	S	T	U	V	W	X	Y	Z	A	B	C	D	E	F	G	H	I	J	K	L	M	N	O	P	Q
S	S	T	U	V	W	X	Y	Z	A	B	C	D	E	F	G	H	I	J	K	L	M	N	O	P	Q	R
T	T	U	V	W	X	Y	Z	A	B	C	D	E	F	G	H	I	J	K	L	M	N	O	P	Q	R	S
U	U	V	W	X	Y	Z	A	B	C	D	E	F	G	H	I	J	K	L	M	N	O	P	Q	R	S	T
V	V	W	X	Y	Z	A	B	C	D	E	F	G	H	I	J	K	L	M	N	O	P	Q	R	S	T	U
W	W	X	Y	Z	A	B	C	D	E	F	G	H	I	J	K	L	M	N	O	P	Q	R	S	T	U	V
X	X	Y	Z	A	B	C	D	E	F	G	H	I	J	K	L	M	N	O	P	Q	R	S	T	U	V	W
Y	Y	Z	A	B	C	D	E	F	G	H	I	J	K	L	M	N	O	P	Q	R	S	T	U	V	W	X
Z	Z	A	B	C	D	E	F	G	H	I	J	K	L	M	N	O	P	Q	R	S	T	U	V	W	X	Y

In the 1500's, the Vigenère cipher, nicknamed "le chiffre indéchiffrable" (French for "the unbreakable cipher") was discovered. It took some time, but, eventually, the unbreakable cipher was broken.

Let's try the message "test tomorrow." To code the first letter, we look for the letter that is at the intersection of the "L" row and the "t" column. Which is the letter E. To code the second letter, use the "l" row and the "e" column to get M. Continuing with the other letters, we get:

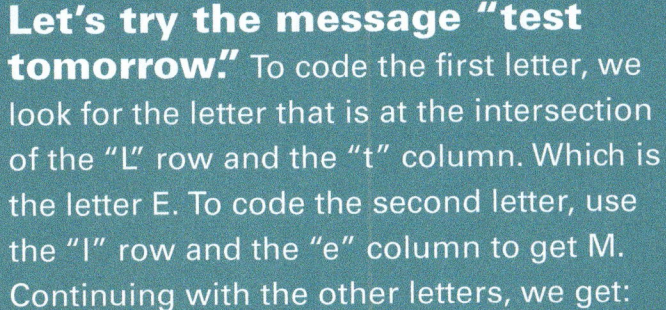

Keyword	L	I	O	N	L	I	O	N	L	I	O	N
Plaintext	t	e	s	t	s	a	t	u	r	d	a	y
Ciphertext	E	M	G	G	D	I	H	H	C	L	O	L

So, "test tomorrow" would be coded "EMGG DIHH CLOL." One of the main advantages of this cipher is that the same letter gets coded into different letters. For example, the "t's" get coded as "E," "G," and "H."

So, this is a hard code to break. And, if you think that someone may have cracked the code, all you must do is change the keyword, and all their work is useless. If instead of using "LION," we had used a longer word like "DISCOVERY," or a keyphrase, like "THISCODEISHARDTOBREAK," the code would be even tougher to break.

So, how was the Vigenère Cipher broken? Essentially, people learned to look for repeated series of letters in the cipher text. Then, using *factoring* (hey, that's math!) and other skills, they made educated guesses as to what the keyword length might be and which Caesar ciphers were being used.

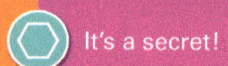

Pirates and buried treasure

Ahoy, matey! Would you like to search for buried treasure? Then you might want to learn about the Pigpen Cipher:

Using the chart, we see that the letter "A" is coded ⌐, the letter "N" is coded ▢, the letter "V" is coded ∧, the letter "Y" is coded <, etc.

While walking on the beach you see a bottle with two pieces of paper in it! The first piece of paper says:

This 'ere next code be called the **Pigpen Cipher.** 'owever, it be not a code that farm animals use. But pirates do for buried treasure!

Arrgh, matey, this looks like nonsense! Could this be the Pigpen Cipher? The first symbol is the same as the "T" in the Pigpen Cipher. The next two are the "H" and the "E." Blimey! That spells the word "The." What about the rest of the message? Shiver me timbers! This message says, "The map leads to Peg Leg(')s loot."

The other page in the bottle has a map with these symbols. Can you read them?

Avast ye! The map says, "X marks the spot". It looks like a treasure is waiting for you! Jolly luck finding Peg Leg's loot!

CURIOUS CONNECTIONS

HISTORY According to legend, when French pirate Olivier Levasseur died in 1730, he left a note using an advanced type of Pigpen Cipher that described where he left a buried treasure. Despite many attempts, the treasure has never been found.

BREAKING CODES

You are out for a walk. Suddenly, you see a piece of paper that was dropped by a spy. Ugh, the message is in a secret code. There is no way you can read the message, right? Wrong! There are tricks you can use to read it.

Throughout history people have used various secret codes to hide the content of messages. For as long as people have been making codes, other people have been trying to break them. After all, knowing other people's secrets could be useful.

Codebreaking skills have even been used to learn how to read ancient languages that nobody has used for centuries, such as Egyptian *hieroglyphics*!

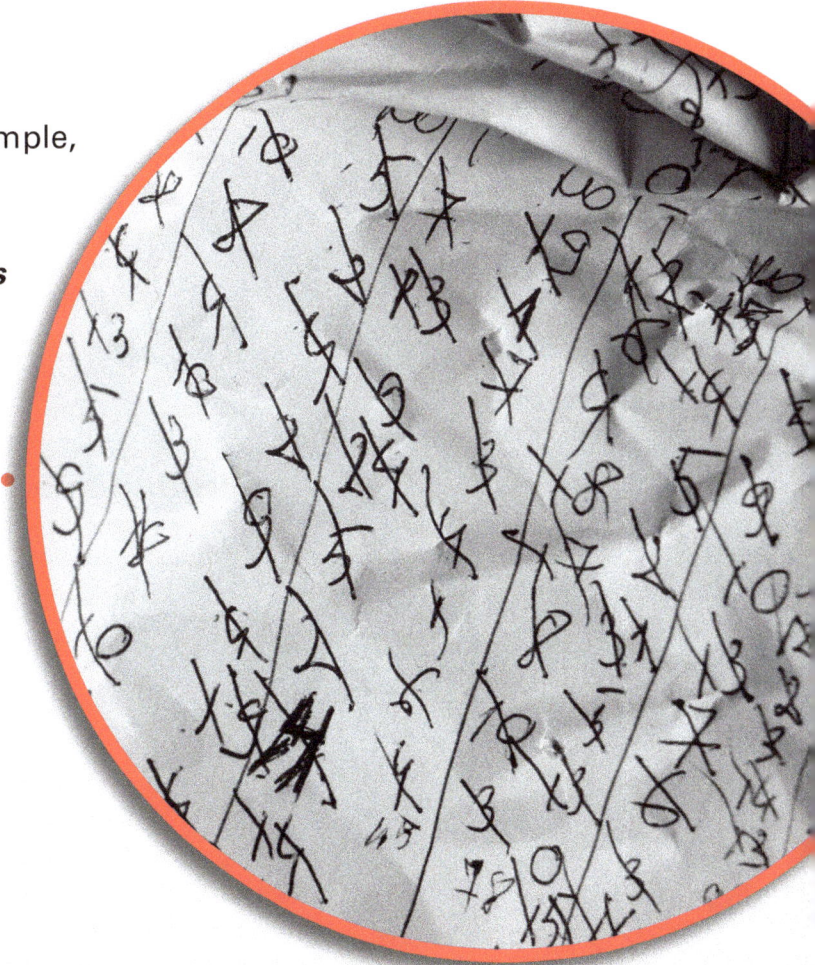

- **Codebreakers use all sorts of math to help them break codes.** For example, they look for *patterns* that might provide clues as to how the code was set up. They also use *statistics* to look for common letters and symbols that might give insights into what they represent.

Of course, it is not easy breaking codes. But, through using math, *logic*, intuition, …. and lots of patience, they can be broken.

Breaking codes

Counting letters

Take any book and turn to a random page. As you read the book, make a frequency chart of the letters. To do this, divide a sheet of paper into two columns. In one column (labelled "Letter") write the letters "a," "b," "c" down to "z." In the other column (labelled "Frequency") tally the number of times you see each letter.

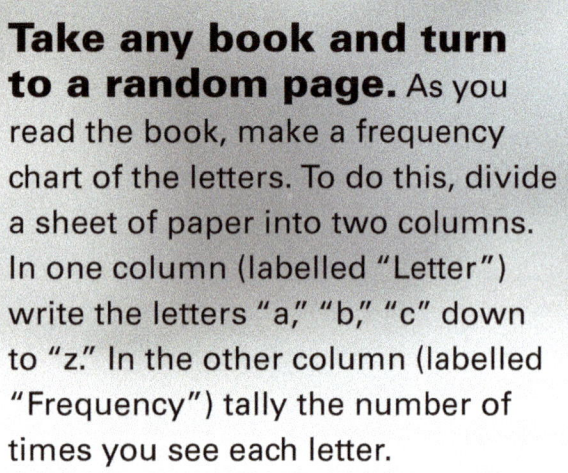

It says "Feed the dog"!

Look at your chart. Do some letters occur more frequently than others? Which ones? In the English language, the letters "e" and "t" generally occur more often than any other letter. Other letters, like "q," "x," and "z" occur infrequently. While we are talking about the English language here, the same is also true for other languages.

Codemakers and codebreakers are always trying to get one step ahead of each other. We have seen how to make codes. Now, let's see how we might break them!

***Cryptanalysts* (people who break codes)** can use letter frequency (called frequency analysis) to help guess at letters and words. For example, if a cryptanalyst saw a coded message that said:

WKP   WCYYF   GCW   GKCLPN   WKP   QMOLP

She would notice that the letters "P" and "W" each occur 4 times, more than any other letters in the coded message. Could these represent "e," "t," or some other common letter? Starting there, she could guess and check to try to figure out the message. This is a very short message, however. Frequency analysis works better with longer messages.

CAREER CORNER

Think breaking codes is fun? You may want to become a cryptanalyst! Cryptanalysts are people who use various methods to try to break secret codes. Elizabeth Friedman was a famous cryptanalyst who broke codes during both world wars.

Reading Caesar's mail

The message you intercepted has a Nelson Mandela quote coded in a Caesar cipher. (Not sure why someone felt the need to code a Mandela message in the first place, but that's all right, it gives us practice.) How could you decode it?

L QHYHU ORVH L HLWKHU ZLQ RU OHDUQ.

Nelson Mandela was the first Black president of South Africa. He had long been a major figure in the struggle for racial justice.

A couple of hints might help. First, the most common letter in the code is "H," which appears 6 times. Maybe "H" is a common letter like "e or "t"? Secondly, the first and fourth words each have only one letter ("L"). The only words in the English language that have one letter are "a" and "i." So, the "L" must represent one of those two letters. A *cryptanalyst* would use information like this to help decode the message.

You've *intercepted* a secret message that you know is using a Caesar cipher. Is there a way you can break the code and figure out what it says? Yep, let's see how!

     e   e   e   e   e   e
L QHYHU ORVH L HLWKHU ZLQ RU OHDUQ

Plaintext	a	b	c	d	e	f	g	h	i	j	k	l	m	n	o	p	q	r	s	t	u	v	w	x	y	z
Ciphertext	D	E	F	G	H	I	J	K	L	M	N	O	P	Q	R	S	T	U	V	W	X	Y	Z	A	B	C

Let's guess that the "H" in the code represents the letter "e." Because "H" is 3 letters to the right of the letter "e," we can make the above Caesar cipher where every letter in the ciphertext is 3 letters to the right of the letter in plaintext. Let's see if this works. Aha, success! When we try the other letters in this Caesar cipher, we get the quote "I never lose, I either win or learn."

You may wonder what would have happened if our initial guess had been wrong. For example, if we had guessed that the ciphertext "H" represented the letter "a" instead? The resulting Caesar cipher would have given us the nonsense quote: "e jaran hkoa e aepdan sej kn hawnj." A cryptanalyst seeing this would know that the initial guess was wrong and would try something else.

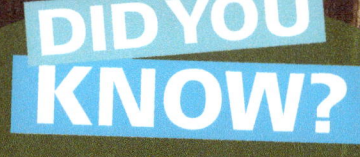

DID YOU KNOW?

How might a codemaker combat frequency analysis? One way is to introduce intentional misspellings. While the codebreaker is thrown off, the person the message was sent to should be able to figure out what words the misspellings represent.

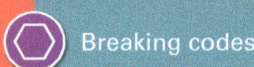
Breaking codes

Read what Tut's friends wrote

The ancient Egyptians used hieroglyphics, a form of writing that used picture symbols, for more than 3,000 years. However, the time came when people stopped writing in hieroglyphs, and nobody knew what the various symbols meant.

Today, you can see the Rosetta stone at the British Museum in London, United Kingdom.

Then, in 1799, a French soldier found a stone (now called the Rosetta stone) buried in the mud near Rosetta, a city near Alexandria, Egypt. The Rosetta stone had writing in three scripts—hieroglyphics, Coptic (an Egyptian language), and Greek. By using methods similar to modern codebreaking techniques, scholars were able to get some insight into what the hieroglyphics meant.

Imagine being an Egyptian *archaeologist*, seeing *hieroglyphs* throughout the country, and having no idea what they said! If only you could read them ....

In 1822, a French scholar named Jean-Francois Champollion figured out the Rosetta stone. Using the Greek text as a guide, Champollion studied the position and repetition of proper names in the Greek text on the stone and was able to pick out the same names in the Egyptian text. Eventually, also using his knowledge of Coptic, Champollion was able to read the whole text on the stone!

By the way, hieroglyphics could be written from left to right, right to left, or top to bottom. So how did the ancient Egyptians know which way to read them? They looked at the animals. If the animals are facing left, then the hieroglyphics would be read from left to right. If the animals are facing right, then they are read from right to left.

CAREER CORNER

Hieroglyphics isn't the only ancient writing that has been *deciphered*. In 1953, Linear B, a system of writing used by the ancient Greeks, was deciphered. Today, archaeologists use codebreaking techniques to try to decipher other ancient languages.

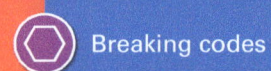
Breaking codes

Codebreakers at war

During World War II (1939-1945), Germany used a device called the Enigma machine to code messages for their troops and spies. The Enigma machine made use of extremely complex *encryption* for its time. Because of this, the code was impossible to break. Or, so the Germans thought!

Eventually, British codebreakers (with help from earlier work done by Polish codebreakers) broke the code by taking advantage of several weaknesses with the Enigma codes.

For example, the Germans sent a weather report every morning that was always formatted the same way. Because the codebreakers knew what certain words were, they could use this information and work backwards to figure out the code. Some historians believe that World War II would have lasted years longer (and killed many more people) if the Enigma machine wasn't cracked.

Codebreaking has changed the course of history! Wars have been won because one side could read the other side's codes. Cracking German codes during World War II gave the Allies a big advantage!

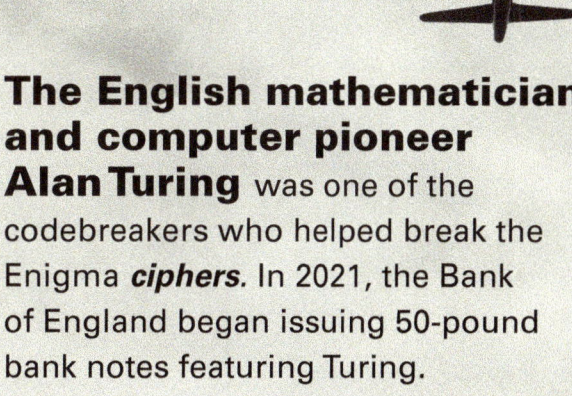

This monument in Poznan, Poland, honors Marian Rejewski and two other Polish codebreakers (whose names are on the other sides of the monument) who helped crack the Enigma code.

The English mathematician and computer pioneer Alan Turing was one of the codebreakers who helped break the Enigma *ciphers*. In 2021, the Bank of England began issuing 50-pound bank notes featuring Turing.

CURIOUS CONNECTIONS

HISTORY During the two world wars, small groups (called code talkers) of Native Americans helped the United States armed forces by developing codes in Native American languages to send secret messages.

CODES AND COMPUTERS

You can find computers in airplanes, in automobiles, in robots, in smartphones, in spacecraft, in televisions, in video game consoles, in watches, and many other devices. Without computers, our world would be vastly different.

Computers are everywhere! In addition to the computers that you use at home or at school, there are also computers in many other devices. And these computers rely on codes!

For computers to work, *programmers* need to write and edit detailed sets of instructions that tell the computer what to do. The process of creating these instructions is called *coding*. In coding, programmers use languages that humans understand that are converted into a language that computers can understand and carry out.

Just as raised dots, the position of flags, or secret messages can represent a message that needs to be **communicated**, so to do these programmer languages represent instructions for the computer to carry out. And that's not the end of codes and computers. Codes can tell cashiers what items you buy at the store and can be used to make your purchase safe. So, read on, to see computers using codes.

DID YOU KNOW?

Your smartphone has more computing power (by a wide margin!) than the computers onboard Apollo 11, which took the first astronauts to the moon!

On July 20, 1969, American astronauts Neil Armstrong and Buzz Aldrin (shown below) became the first people to step on the moon.

Oh, yeah! Let's see your smartphone get you to the moon!

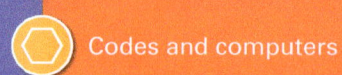

Codes and computers

Talking to your computer

Every number you have probably ever seen has used the *decimal* system. The decimal system, or base 10, uses 10 digits—0 through 9. You are probably so familiar with the decimal system that you don't realize that you are using it. And, you may wonder how any other system could even exist?

Leibniz developed the binary number system, or base 2, which uses only two digits, generally 0 and 1. You can convert numbers from the decimal system to the binary system, or vice versa. For example:

Binary Number	Decimal Number
101	5
10110	22
100000	32
1011011	91

In the late 1600's German mathematician Gottfried Wilhelm Leibniz developed the *binary* number system that was ignored for centuries! That is, until computers were invented.

So, what does the binary number system have to do with computers? A computer processes information in the form of data. Computers represent data using codes of 0's and 1's. So, computers represent numbers, words, images, sounds, and virtually any other kind of information as long sequences of 0's and 1's.

When *programmers* write instructions for the computers, they don't just write line after line of 0's and 1's. Instead, they write instructions in a language that humans can understand, which is *coded* into a series of 0's and 1's that the computer can understand.

This ancient Babylonian tablet, which shows a use for geometry, is over 3,500 years old! The Babylonians' base 60 number system is still used today. The reason there are 60 seconds in a minute, 60 minutes in an hour, and 360 degrees in a circle is because of their system.

CURIOUS CONNECTIONS

HISTORY While we are used to the base 10 number system, other number systems have been used, and are still being used, throughout the world. The Celts and Mayans used a base-20 system, the Oksapmin people of Papua New Guinea use a base 27 system, and the ancient Babylonians used a base 60 system.

Codes and computers

Codes at the store

Next time you are at the grocery store (or any other store for that matter), look closely at the food. Do you see a series of lines with numbers underneath them? That series of lines and numbers is called the barcode.

We can think of the barcode like the other codes we have seen so far. Just like a series of raised dots represent a letter in Braille or a series of letters represent a message in a secret code, so, too, do the bars, lines, and digits represent the product. At a store's checkout counter, a scanner reads barcodes by beaming a light across the code and interpreting it as a series of numbers. The store's computer uses the sequence of numbers to search a database for product information. It relays the item's price and other information to the cashier.

A barcode consists of a pattern of bars and lines that a computer can change into information about an item. The digits or other characters contain the same information as the bars and lines.

Beep! Beep! Beep! At the grocery store, you see the cashier scanning the barcode on each item you buy. Why don't they just type the price into the register?

So, why use the barcode and not just enter the price for each item? Barcodes make it easier to change the prices of items when they go on or off sale, and they help stores keep track of inventory. Barcodes also give prices more quickly than cashiers can enter them, and eliminate the possibility of the cashier entering the incorrect price.

TECH TIME

One type of barcode is a QR (Quick Response) code. A QR code is a grid **pattern** that can be scanned with a cell phone's camera, typically causing the phone to display a web page.

41

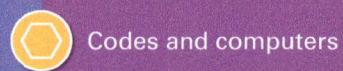

Codes and computers

Are credit cards **safe**?

So, what do codes and secret messages have to do with using credit cards? When you send a secret message, you need to change it from the original message, called plaintext, to a coded message, called ciphertext. **Encryption** is the procedure that changes a message to disguise it. This is good for the recipient who knows how to turn the ciphertext back into plaintext. Encryption is bad for someone who **intercepts** the message but has no idea what it means.

CAREER CORNER

If you like computers and codes, you may want to become a cryptographer! Cryptographers help keep computers safe by writing algorithms that hackers can't break … at least not easily.

You just used barcodes to help you ring up your groceries. Now, it is time to pay for them. How do stores make sure that credit cards are safe to use?

Many credit cards have an EMV chip on them. (EMV stands for Europay, Mastercard, and Visa.) The EMV chip, which contains the cardholder's information, makes credit cards more secure.

To keep your credit card information safe, stores encrypt the credit card number and other personal information. An *algorithm* (step-by-step mathematical procedure) scrambles the credit card number into a sort of secret code.

Only those authorized to view the information can turn the secret code back into the customer's credit card number. If a hacker intercepts the data, they just get a mess of characters that make no sense to them.

43

Write like Tut!

You will need:
- Pencil
- Paper

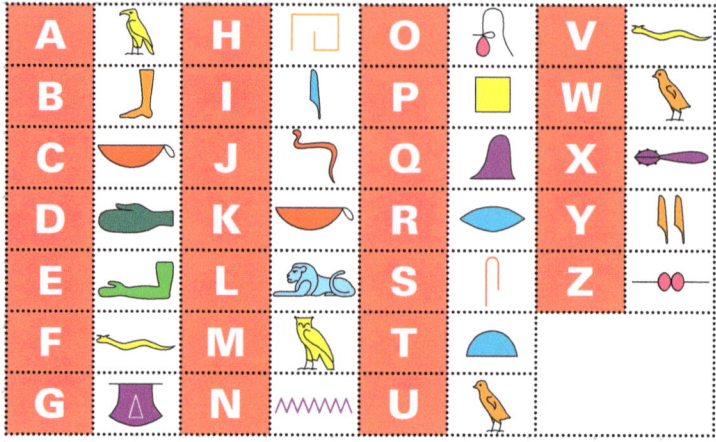

You, too, can be an archaeologist! Use this chart to read the hieroglyphics on these pages.

Imagine you are an archaeologist working in ancient Egypt. You see this cartouche (an oval ring with a person's name in it). Can you figure out the pharaoh (ancient Egyptian king) whose name is in the cartouche? To help you out a little, the "chick" symbols that are in the cartouches on this page represent the letter "u," not the letter "w."

The first letter (the bowl) can either be "C" or "K." The second symbol represents the letter "h." The third and fifth symbols (the chicks) both represent the letter "u." The fourth symbol (the snake) represents the letter "f." So, the name in the cartouche is either "Chufu" or "Khufu." Hey, wait a minute … there was a pharaoh named Khufu. In fact, the Great Pyramid at Giza was built as his tomb!

Have you ever dreamed of being an archaeologist and learning more about ancient civilizations? Archaeologists working in Egypt need to know how to read hieroglyphics. Let's see if you can read (and write) like an ancient Egyptian!

Give it a try

OK, now it is your turn. See if you can figure out the pharaoh whose name is in this cartouche. (Again, remember the chicks represent the letter "u.")

You should have gotten "Tutankhamun," also known as the famous "King Tut."

Try this next!

See if you can figure out the pharaohs whose names are in these cartouches. To help you out, the cup represents the letter "c" and the chick represents the letter "u."

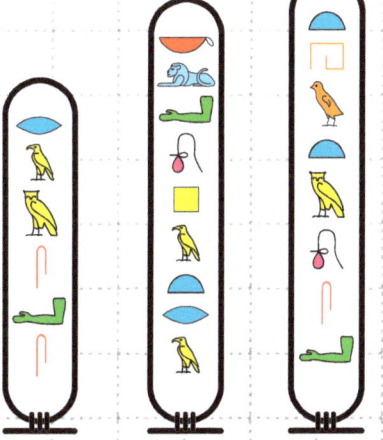

These cartouches contain the names of Ramses, Cleopatra, and Thutmose.

QUESTION TIME!

Can you write your name in hieroglyphics? Write the names of some famous people in hieroglyphics and see if a friend can figure out who they are. Have a friend write the names of some famous people and see if you can figure out who they are.

45

Index

A
Aldrin, Buzz, 37
algorithms, 42-43
A1Z26 cipher, 16-17, 21
Apollo 11 (spacecraft), 37
archaeologists, 33, 44-45
Armstrong, Neil, 37
Atbash cipher, 17, 21

B
Babylonians, 39
barcodes, 40-41
base 20 number system, 39
base 27 number system, 39
base 60 number system, 39
binary number system, 38-39
Bonaparte, Napoleon, 12
Braille, 8-9, 40
Braille, Louis, 8

C
Caesar, Julius, 18
Caesar cipher, 18-23, 30-31
Carter, Howard, 45
cartouches, 44-45
Celts, 39
Champollion, Jean-Francois, 33
Chappe, Claude, 12-13
ciphers, 15-25, 30-31, 35
code talkers, 35

codebreaking, 5, 27, 29, 31-35
codemaking, 5, 29, 31
coding, on computers, 37
Coptic language, 32-33
credit cards, 42-43
cryptanalysts, 29-31
cryptography (career), 43
currency, 9

D
decimal number system, 38

E
Egypt, ancient, 32-33, 44-45
EMV chips, 42
encryption, 34, 42
Enigma machine, 34-35

F
factoring, 23
Friedman, Elizabeth, 29

G
Great Pyramid at Giza, 44
Greece, ancient, 19, 33
Greek language, 32-33

H
hieroglyphs, 27, 32-33, 44-45
Holmes, Sherlock, 21

K
Khufu (pharaoh), 44

L
Leibniz, Gottfried Wilhelm, 38-39
Levasseur, Olivier, 25
Linear B (writing system), 33
logic, 27

M
Mandela, Nelson, 30
Mayans, 39
Morse, Samuel F. B., 10
Morse code, 10-11
Morse Glasses, 11

O
Oksapmin people, 39

P
patterns, 8, 27, 40-41
peace sign, 13
Pigpen cipher, 24-25
pirates, 14, 24-25
programmers, 5, 37, 39

Q
QR (Quick Response) codes, 41

R
radio signals, 10
Rejewski, Marian, 25
Rosetta stone, 32-33

S
scytales, 19
semaphore, 13
smartphones, 36-37
statistics, 27
substitution, 16-17, 20-21

T
Titanic (ship), 11
towers, used to send messages, 12-13
Turing, Alan, 35
Tutankhamun (King Tut), 45

V
Vigenère cipher, 22-23

W
World War II, 29, 34-35

Glossary

algorithm (AL guh rihth uhm)—a step-by-step procedure for solving a mathematical problem

archaeologist (AHR kee OL uh jihst)—a person who studies people, customs, and life of ancient times

binary (BY nuhr ee) number system—a numbering system that uses 2 digits—usually 0 and 1. The system groups numbers by twos and powers of two.

cipher (SY fuhr)—a secret writing or code

coding—the process of creating instructions that a computer can carry out

communicate (kuh MYOO nuh kayt)—to give information by speaking or writing; to exchange ideas or thoughts

cryptanalyst (krihp TAN uh lihst)—a person who breaks and deciphers coded messages

decimal (DEHS uh muhl) number system—a numbering system that uses 10 digits—0 through 9. The system groups numbers by tens and powers of ten.

decipher (dih SY fuhr)—to make out the meaning of something that is not clear

efficient (uh FIHSH uhnt)—able to produce the effect wanted without waste of time or energy

encryption (ehn KRIHP shuhn)—a procedure that changes a message to disguise it

factoring (FAK tuhr ihng)—determining what numbers when multiplied together give you a different number

hieroglyphic (HY uhr uh GLIHF ihk)—a picture, character, or symbol standing for a word, idea, or sound

intercept (IHN tuhr SEHPT)—to take or seize on the way from one place to another

logic (LOJ ihk)—the art of reasoning

pattern (PAT uhrn)—any arrangement; the structure or design of a work

practical (PRAK tuh kuhl)—fit for actual practice; useful

programmer (PROH gram uhr)—a person who writes and codes the instructions which control the work of a computer or other automatic machine

radio (RAY dee oh)—the way of sending and receiving words, music, and other sounds by electric waves, without wires

statistics (stuh TIHS tihks)—the branch of mathematics that deals with collecting and analyzing data

www.ingramcontent.com/pod-product-compliance
Lightning Source LLC
Chambersburg PA
CBHW061250170426
43191CB00041B/2407